D1309084

Dinosaur Digs

Discovering Brachiosaurus

Written by Rena Korb
Illustrated by Ted Dawson

Content Consultant:
Kenneth Carpenter
Curator of Lower Vertebrate Paleontology & Chief Preparator
Denver Museum of Nature and Science

magic
Wagon

ANDERSON COUNTY LIBRARY
ANDERSON, S.C.

visit us at www.abdopublishing.com

Published by Magic Wagon, a division of the ABDO Publishing Group, 8000 West 78th Street, Edina, Minnesota 55439. Copyright © 2008 by Abdo Consulting Group, Inc. International copyrights reserved in all countries. All rights reserved. No part of this book may be reproduced in any form without written permission from the publisher.

Looking Glass Library™ is a trademark and logo of Magic Wagon.

Printed in the United States.

Text by Rena Korb
Illustrations by Ted Dawson
Edited by Jill Sherman
Interior layout and design by Emily Love
Cover design by Emily Love

Library of Congress Cataloging-in-Publication Data
Korb, Rena B.
  Discovering brachiosaurus / Rena Korb ; illustrated by Ted Dawson ; content consultant, Kenneth Carpenter.
     p. cm. — (Dinosaur digs)
  Includes bibliographical references.
  ISBN 978-1-60270-105-2 (alk. paper)
  1. Brachiosaurus—Juvenile literature. I. Dawson, Ted, ill. II. Title.
QE862.S3K66 2008
567.913—dc22
                        2007034041

FOSSIL FINDS

The first *Brachiosaurus* (BRA-kee-oh-sor-uhs) fossil was uncovered in 1883 in Canon City, Colorado. At first, paleontologists thought it belonged to *Brontosaurus*. The bone was even used to construct a full *Brontosaurus* skeleton. The fossil was not identified as *Brachiosaurus* until 1998.

Seven years after the Colorado discovery, Elmer Riggs found a leg bone and ribs in Colorado. After studying these fossils, he named *Brachiosaurus* in 1903.

The greatest *Brachiosaurus* discovery occurred between 1907 and 1912 in Tanzania, Africa. German paleontologists dug up huge bones they found near a place called Tendaguru. They soon discovered that among the bones were those of *Brachiosaurus*. Over the next few years, workers dug thousands of fossils from the ground. The *Brachiosaurus* skeleton was sent to Germany. The fossil is being stored at the Humbolt Museum of Natural History in Berlin.

Hong had a lot of good memories of dinosaur hunting with his father. He had helped discover fossils in the desert. He had helped dig bones out of rocky cliffs. He had even helped unearth dinosaurs that the world had never seen before. One of Hong's favorite memories was when his father, a paleontologist, found a dinosaur footprint.

Hong had never seen a fossilized footprint before. He saw that the toes went deeper into the ground than the heels.

"What does that mean?" asked his father.

Hong thought for a moment. Then, he had the answer! "It means that the dinosaur walked forward, on its toes, not on its heels," he said.

Hong had spent the rest of the afternoon walking like a dinosaur.

Now, Hong had a chance to make a new memory. He and his father were joining a dig in a country in eastern Africa called Tanzania. The workers had uncovered hundreds of dinosaur bones. They'd even found the leg bone of a *Brachiosaurus!* The scientists hoped the dig would uncover more of the skeleton.

Brachiosaurus was one of the largest dinosaurs to ever walk the earth. Its neck alone stretched 30 feet (9 m). Hong pictured the dinosaur with legs as large as tree trunks, peeking into a fourth-story window.

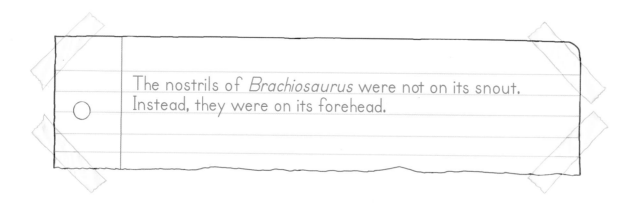

The nostrils of *Brachiosaurus* were not on its snout. Instead, they were on its forehead.

The largest *Brachiosaurus* may have weighed 50 tons (45 t). But most likely, it weighed much less than that. Hong knew he was one lucky dinosaur hunter.

About 150 million years ago, Tanzania had been home to a busy animal community. An earlier dig in Tanzania at Tendaguru had unearthed bones from large and small dinosaurs, flying reptiles, sharks, and fish.

Hong was excited to be going to the same site as that important discovery. He hoped that the dig he and his father were about to join would be as exciting.

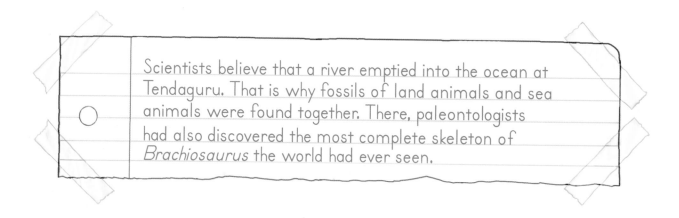

Scientists believe that a river emptied into the ocean at Tendaguru. That is why fossils of land animals and sea animals were found together. There, paleontologists had also discovered the most complete skeleton of *Brachiosaurus* the world had ever seen.

Hong became even more excited on the ride to the dig's camp. His eyes took in the rolling grasslands thickly covered with trees and shrubs. He knew then that this was going to be a very different kind of dig. Most dinosaur fossils in the United States were removed from hard rock. He hoped he might learn something new.

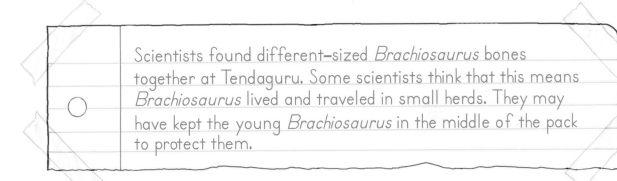

Scientists found different-sized *Brachiosaurus* bones together at Tendaguru. Some scientists think that this means *Brachiosaurus* lived and traveled in small herds. They may have kept the young *Brachiosaurus* in the middle of the pack to protect them.

When Hong arrived, he was eager to jump in. People were hard at work around long holes in the earth. They were carefully uncovering the fossils.

Some people used shovels to dig the pits and make them even bigger. Others carried large bones wrapped in plaster to trucks waiting to haul them away. Still others examined large bones or used tools to clear away the soft rock.

"They are digging pits to find dinosaur bones," Hong's father said. "But how do they know where to dig?"

Hong thought. Soon the words of a famous paleontologist jumped into his head. Hong replied, "Dig where you see a fossil! A bone must have been poking out of the rock."

"That's right," said Hong's father. "Rain and wind wore down the soft rock until people could see the buried bones."

The next day, Hong grabbed his backpack filled with tools and followed his father to the biggest pit. Workers already had found several *Brachiosaurus* bones, but much work remained. After all, *Brachiosaurus* was longer than an 18-wheel truck and weighed many tons more.

Brachiosaurus bones were large! It would take a lot of work to collect all the bones. And each bone had to be protected and packed up to send to the museum.

The pit buzzed with activity. Several people were working on a map that showed how the bones lying in the pit had been found. Hong knew that by studying the position of the bones, paleontologists could learn more about the dinosaur. They could get a better idea about how the bones fit together and how the dinosaur died.

Some people used machines to take the bones from the earth, where they had rested for millions of years.

Others searched for smaller fossils that had been overlooked. If these pieces fit into the larger bones, they could be glued in place later.

Hong peered into the pit where workers cleaned off a jumble of *Brachiosaurus* bones. Hong saw the bones of the ribs. They were longer than three of him!

Hong saw what must be a leg bone. Just one bone stretched seven feet (2 m) long. He saw several bones that made up the dinosaur's foot. With one step, *Brachiosaurus* could easily stomp on anything in its way—including him!

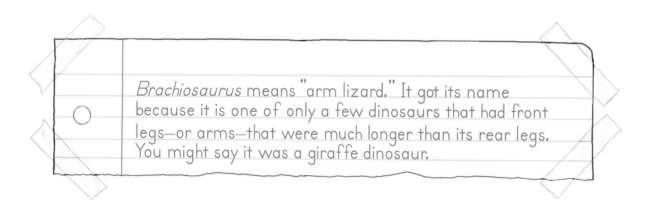

Brachiosaurus means "arm lizard." It got its name because it is one of only a few dinosaurs that had front legs—or arms—that were much longer than its rear legs. You might say it was a giraffe dinosaur.

One worker studied the skull. It was so small next to the rest of the bones. Hong laughed to himself. Imagine thinking a skull almost two feet (.6 m) long was small!

The woman waved and moved aside to give him a better look. Now, Hong could even see a few of the teeth in the skull. *Brachiosaurus* was an herbivore and probably spent most of the day using these teeth to nip leaves from high in the treetops. It would have had to in order to keep its enormous body nourished. A *Brachiosaurus* stomach could hold about 500 pounds (227 kg) of food.

Brachiosaurus did not chew its food. It swallowed leaves and fruits whole. It may have also swallowed stones to help break up the food.

Hong's father interrupted his thoughts when he asked, "Have you looked around enough? Are you ready to get to work?"

"You bet!" Hong replied.

Hong and his father jumped into a shallow pit next to a neck bone. Before getting started, Hong pulled out his field notebook. He wrote down information about the bone and drew a picture of it. He pulled out his tape measure, which showed his guess had been right. Just this one neck bone measured three feet (1 m) long!

Over the next few hours, Hong and his father cleaned that bone. They used small brushes to remove loose dirt. They used pointy awls to pry away dirt that had hardened onto the bone. But, they never let their tools touch the bone. They were careful not to damage the fossil.

Finally, it was time to prepare the bone to be moved. Hong wrapped it in newspaper. Then, he soaked wide strips of burlap in plaster. He wrapped the burlap around the fossil until it looked like a big loaf of bread. When it dried, workers would load it on the truck.

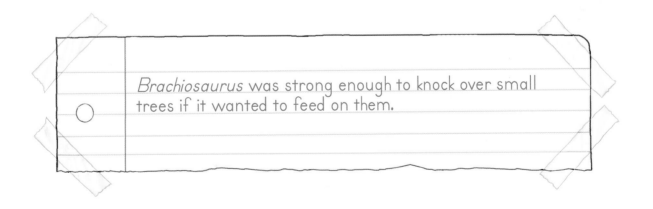

Brachiosaurus was strong enough to knock over small trees if it wanted to feed on them.

Hong sat down and thought about how many hours he had spent working on just one bone. He did not mind. *Brachiosaurus* had died millions of years ago, but the dinosaur was not gone forever. Hong had helped bring one really big dinosaur back to life. He knew that people who visited the skeleton at the museum would be as amazed as he had been when he first laid eyes on *Brachiosaurus*.

"Hong!" his father called. "Ready to start again?"

"Sure," he said, running to the next bone.

ACTIVITY: Tools for Digging

What does a paleontologist use these tools for?

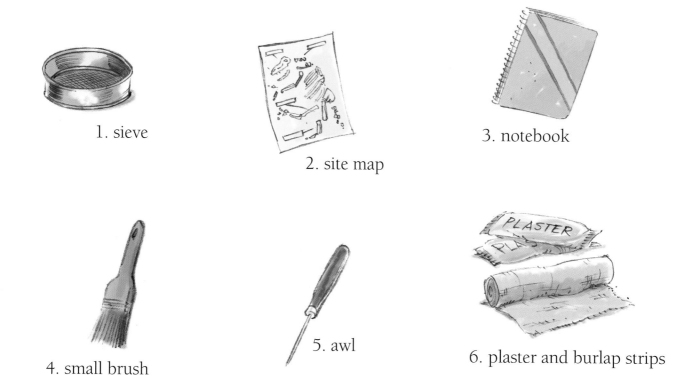

1. sieve

2. site map

3. notebook

4. small brush

5. awl

6. plaster and burlap strips

ANSWERS:
1. to help paleontologists find small fossils that have been overlooked; 2. to tell paleontologists how the bones were laying; 3. to write down notes about fossils; 4. to remove loose dirt from bones; 5. to scrape away dirt from bones; 6. to wrap up bones for moving

GLOSSARY

awl — a tool with a sharp point.

dig — a place where scientists try to recover buried objects by digging.

fossil — the remains of an animal or a plant from a past age, such as a skeleton or a footprint, that has been preserved in the earth or a rock.

grassland — land on which grass or low green plants are the main plant life.

herbivore — an animal that eats grass and other plants.

nourish — to eat enough food to be kept healthy.

paleontologist — (pay-lee-ahn-TAH-luh-jist) a person who studies fossils and ancient animals and plants.

shallow — not deep.

LANDER JUVNONFICT
26606574
J 567.913 Korb Rena
Korb, Rena B.
Discovering brachiosaurus /

NO LONGER PROPERTY OF
ANDERSON COUNTY LIBRARY

READING LIST

Dalla Vecchia, Fabio Marco. *Brachiosaurus*. San Diego, CA: Blackbirch Press, 2004.
Dixon, Dougal. *The Search for Dinosaurs*. New York: Thomson Learning, 1995.
Lambert, David. *Dinosaur Encyclopedia*. New York: Dorling Kindersley, 2001.

ON THE WEB

To learn more about *Brachiosaurus*, visit ABDO Publishing Company on the World Wide Web at **www.abdopublishing.com**. Web sites about *Brachiosaurus* are featured on our Book Links page. These links are routinely monitored and updated to provide the most current information available.